RED TEAM PLANNER

IF FOUND PLEASE CONTACT:

____

____

____

NETMUX

ISBN-10: 0692111867
ISBN-13: 978-0692111864

	JANUARY	FEBRUARY	MARCH
1			
2			
3			
4			
5			
6			
7			
8			
9			
10			
11			
12			
13			
14			
15			
16			
17			
18			
19			
20			
21			
22			
23			
24			
25			
26			
27			
28			
29			
30			
31			

	APRIL	MAY	JUNE
1			
2			
3			
4			
5			
6			
7			
8			
9			
10			
11			
12			
13			
14			
15			
16			
17			
18			
19			
20			
21			
22			
23			
24			
25			
26			
27			
28			
29			
30			
31			

	JULY	AUGUST	SEPTEMBER
1			
2			
3			
4			
5			
6			
7			
8			
9			
10			
11			
12			
13			
14			
15			
16			
17			
18			
19			
20			
21			
22			
23			
24			
25			
26			
27			
28			
29			
30			
31			

	OCTOBER	NOVEMBER	DECEMBER
1			
2			
3			
4			
5			
6			
7			
8			
9			
10			
11			
12			
13			
14			
15			
16			
17			
18			
19			
20			
21			
22			
23			
24			
25			
26			
27			
28			
29			
30			
31			

/CUSTOMER >

POC

POC

POC

/DOCS

☐ NDA ☐ SOW ☐ ROE ☐ Approval ☐ 3rd Party ☐

/ENGAGEMENT

TYPE	SCOPE		TIMELINE
☐ Black Box	☐ Physical	☐ App	From:
	☐ Remote	☐ SocialEng	To:
☐ White Box	☐ Full-Spec	☐ RogueDevice	Status Updates:
	☐ Wireless	☐ Insider	_Daily _Weekly
☐ Grey Box	☐ WebApp	☐ DoS	_Monthly _Quarter

/CUSTOMER INFRASTRUCTURE

/TEST ACCOUNTS

/OBJECTIVES

/NOTES

/TEAM DATA

/TASKS

MEMBER	DESCRIPTION	FIN
		☐
		☐
		☐
		☐
		☐
		☐
		☐
		☐
		☐
		☐
		☐
		☐
		☐
		☐

/TOOLS

DATE	TYPE	NAME	DEPLOY LOCATION

/TEAM INFRASTRUCTURE

TYPE	IP/DOMAIN	USER/PASS

/TEAM ACCOUNTS

SERVICE	USERNAME	PASSWORD

/FINDINGS

/RECOMMENDATIONS

/CUSTOMER >

POC

POC

POC

/DOCS

☐ NDA ☐ SOW ☐ ROE ☐ Approval ☐ 3rd Party ☐

/ENGAGEMENT

TYPE	SCOPE		TIMELINE
☐ Black Box	☐ Physical	☐ App	From:
	☐ Remote	☐ SocialEng	To:
☐ White Box	☐ Full-Spec	☐ RogueDevice	Status Updates:
	☐ Wireless	☐ Insider	_Daily _Weekly
☐ Grey Box	☐ WebApp	☐ DoS	_Monthly _Quarter

/CUSTOMER INFRASTRUCTURE

/TEST ACCOUNTS

/OBJECTIVES

/NOTES

/TEAM DATA

/TASKS

MEMBER	DESCRIPTION	FIN
		☐
		☐
		☐
		☐
		☐
		☐
		☐
		☐
		☐
		☐
		☐
		☐
		☐
		☐

/TOOLS

DATE	TYPE	NAME	DEPLOY LOCATION

/TEAM INFRASTRUCTURE

TYPE	IP/DOMAIN	USER/PASS

/TEAM ACCOUNTS

SERVICE	USERNAME	PASSWORD

/FINDINGS

/RECOMMENDATIONS

/CUSTOMER >

POC

POC

POC

/DOCS

☐ NDA ☐ SOW ☐ ROE ☐ Approval ☐ 3rd Party ☐

/ENGAGEMENT

TYPE	SCOPE		TIMELINE
☐ Black Box	☐ Physical	☐ App	From:
	☐ Remote	☐ SocialEng	To:
☐ White Box	☐ Full-Spec	☐ RogueDevice	Status Updates:
	☐ Wireless	☐ Insider	_Daily _Weekly
☐ Grey Box	☐ WebApp	☐ DoS	_Monthly _Quarter

/CUSTOMER INFRASTRUCTURE

/TEST ACCOUNTS

/OBJECTIVES

/NOTES

/TEAM DATA

/TASKS

MEMBER	DESCRIPTION	FIN
		☐
		☐
		☐
		☐
		☐
		☐
		☐
		☐
		☐
		☐
		☐
		☐
		☐
		☐

/TOOLS

DATE	TYPE	NAME	DEPLOY LOCATION

/TEAM INFRASTRUCTURE

TYPE	IP/DOMAIN	USER/PASS

/TEAM ACCOUNTS

SERVICE	USERNAME	PASSWORD

/FINDINGS

/RECOMMENDATIONS

/CUSTOMER >

POC

POC

POC

/DOCS

☐ NDA ☐ SOW ☐ ROE ☐ Approval ☐ 3rd Party ☐

/ENGAGEMENT

TYPE	SCOPE		TIMELINE
☐ Black Box	☐ Physical	☐ App	From:
	☐ Remote	☐ SocialEng	To:
☐ White Box	☐ Full-Spec	☐ RogueDevice	Status Updates:
	☐ Wireless	☐ Insider	_Daily _Weekly
☐ Grey Box	☐ WebApp	☐ DoS	_Monthly _Quarter

/CUSTOMER INFRASTRUCTURE

/TEST ACCOUNTS

/OBJECTIVES

/NOTES

/TEAM DATA

/TASKS

MEMBER	DESCRIPTION	FIN
		☐
		☐
		☐
		☐
		☐
		☐
		☐
		☐
		☐
		☐
		☐
		☐
		☐
		☐

/TOOLS

DATE	TYPE	NAME	DEPLOY LOCATION

/TEAM INFRASTRUCTURE

TYPE	IP/DOMAIN	USER/PASS

/TEAM ACCOUNTS

SERVICE	USERNAME	PASSWORD

/FINDINGS

/RECOMMENDATIONS

/CUSTOMER >

POC

POC

POC

/DOCS

☐ NDA ☐ SOW ☐ ROE ☐ Approval ☐ 3rd Party ☐

/ENGAGEMENT

TYPE	SCOPE		TIMELINE
☐ Black Box	☐ Physical	☐ App	From:
	☐ Remote	☐ SocialEng	To:
☐ White Box	☐ Full-Spec	☐ RogueDevice	Status Updates:
	☐ Wireless	☐ Insider	_Daily _Weekly
☐ Grey Box	☐ WebApp	☐ DoS	_Monthly _Quarter

/CUSTOMER INFRASTRUCTURE

/TEST ACCOUNTS

/OBJECTIVES

/NOTES

/TEAM DATA

/TASKS

MEMBER	DESCRIPTION	FIN
		☐
		☐
		☐
		☐
		☐
		☐
		☐
		☐
		☐
		☐
		☐
		☐
		☐
		☐

/TOOLS

DATE	TYPE	NAME	DEPLOY LOCATION

/TEAM INFRASTRUCTURE

TYPE	IP/DOMAIN	USER/PASS

/TEAM ACCOUNTS

SERVICE	USERNAME	PASSWORD

/FINDINGS

/RECOMMENDATIONS

/CUSTOMER >

POC

POC

POC

/DOCS

☐ NDA ☐ SOW ☐ ROE ☐ Approval ☐ 3rd Party ☐

/ENGAGEMENT

TYPE	SCOPE		TIMELINE
☐ Black Box	☐ Physical	☐ App	From:
	☐ Remote	☐ SocialEng	To:
☐ White Box	☐ Full-Spec	☐ RogueDevice	Status Updates:
	☐ Wireless	☐ Insider	_Daily _Weekly
☐ Grey Box	☐ WebApp	☐ DoS	_Monthly _Quarter

/CUSTOMER INFRASTRUCTURE

/TEST ACCOUNTS

/OBJECTIVES

/NOTES

/TEAM DATA

/TASKS

MEMBER	DESCRIPTION	FIN
		☐
		☐
		☐
		☐
		☐
		☐
		☐
		☐
		☐
		☐
		☐
		☐
		☐
		☐

/TOOLS

DATE	TYPE	NAME	DEPLOY LOCATION

/TEAM INFRASTRUCTURE

TYPE	IP/DOMAIN	USER/PASS

/TEAM ACCOUNTS

SERVICE	USERNAME	PASSWORD

/FINDINGS

/RECOMMENDATIONS

/CUSTOMER >

POC

POC

POC

/DOCS

☐ NDA ☐ SOW ☐ ROE ☐ Approval ☐ 3rd Party ☐

/ENGAGEMENT

TYPE	SCOPE		TIMELINE
☐ Black Box	☐ Physical	☐ App	From:
	☐ Remote	☐ SocialEng	To:
☐ White Box	☐ Full-Spec	☐ RogueDevice	Status Updates:
	☐ Wireless	☐ Insider	_Daily _Weekly
☐ Grey Box	☐ WebApp	☐ DoS	_Monthly _Quarter

/CUSTOMER INFRASTRUCTURE

/TEST ACCOUNTS

/OBJECTIVES

/NOTES

/TEAM DATA

/TASKS

MEMBER	DESCRIPTION	FIN
		☐
		☐
		☐
		☐
		☐
		☐
		☐
		☐
		☐
		☐
		☐
		☐
		☐
		☐

/TOOLS

DATE	TYPE	NAME	DEPLOY LOCATION

/TEAM INFRASTRUCTURE

TYPE	IP/DOMAIN	USER/PASS

/TEAM ACCOUNTS

SERVICE	USERNAME	PASSWORD

/FINDINGS

/RECOMMENDATIONS

/CUSTOMER >

POC

POC

POC

/DOCS

☐ NDA ☐ SOW ☐ ROE ☐ Approval ☐ 3rd Party ☐

/ENGAGEMENT

TYPE	SCOPE		TIMELINE
☐ Black Box	☐ Physical	☐ App	From:
	☐ Remote	☐ SocialEng	To:
☐ White Box	☐ Full-Spec	☐ RogueDevice	Status Updates:
	☐ Wireless	☐ Insider	_Daily _Weekly
☐ Grey Box	☐ WebApp	☐ DoS	_Monthly _Quarter

/CUSTOMER INFRASTRUCTURE

/TEST ACCOUNTS

/OBJECTIVES

/NOTES

/TEAM DATA

/TASKS

MEMBER	DESCRIPTION	FIN
		☐
		☐
		☐
		☐
		☐
		☐
		☐
		☐
		☐
		☐
		☐
		☐
		☐
		☐

/TOOLS

DATE	TYPE	NAME	DEPLOY LOCATION

/TEAM INFRASTRUCTURE

TYPE	IP/DOMAIN	USER/PASS

/TEAM ACCOUNTS

SERVICE	USERNAME	PASSWORD

/FINDINGS

/RECOMMENDATIONS

/CUSTOMER >

POC

POC

POC

/DOCS

☐ NDA ☐ SOW ☐ ROE ☐ Approval ☐ 3rd Party ☐

/ENGAGEMENT

TYPE	SCOPE		TIMELINE
☐ Black Box	☐ Physical	☐ App	From:
	☐ Remote	☐ SocialEng	To:
☐ White Box	☐ Full-Spec	☐ RogueDevice	Status Updates:
	☐ Wireless	☐ Insider	_Daily _Weekly
☐ Grey Box	☐ WebApp	☐ DoS	_Monthly _Quarter

/CUSTOMER INFRASTRUCTURE

/TEST ACCOUNTS

/OBJECTIVES

/NOTES

/TEAM DATA

/TASKS

MEMBER	DESCRIPTION	FIN
		☐
		☐
		☐
		☐
		☐
		☐
		☐
		☐
		☐
		☐
		☐
		☐
		☐
		☐

/TOOLS

DATE	TYPE	NAME	DEPLOY LOCATION

/TEAM INFRASTRUCTURE

TYPE	IP/DOMAIN	USER/PASS

/TEAM ACCOUNTS

SERVICE	USERNAME	PASSWORD

/FINDINGS

/RECOMMENDATIONS

/CUSTOMER >

POC

POC

POC

/DOCS

☐ NDA ☐ SOW ☐ ROE ☐ Approval ☐ 3rd Party ☐

/ENGAGEMENT

TYPE	SCOPE		TIMELINE
☐ Black Box	☐ Physical	☐ App	From:
	☐ Remote	☐ SocialEng	To:
☐ White Box	☐ Full-Spec	☐ RogueDevice	Status Updates:
	☐ Wireless	☐ Insider	_Daily _Weekly
☐ Grey Box	☐ WebApp	☐ DoS	_Monthly _Quarter

/CUSTOMER INFRASTRUCTURE

/TEST ACCOUNTS

/OBJECTIVES

/NOTES

/TEAM DATA

/TASKS

MEMBER	DESCRIPTION	FIN
		☐
		☐
		☐
		☐
		☐
		☐
		☐
		☐
		☐
		☐
		☐
		☐
		☐
		☐

/TOOLS

DATE	TYPE	NAME	DEPLOY LOCATION

/TEAM INFRASTRUCTURE

TYPE	IP/DOMAIN	USER/PASS

/TEAM ACCOUNTS

SERVICE	USERNAME	PASSWORD

/FINDINGS

/RECOMMENDATIONS

/CUSTOMER >

POC

POC

POC

/DOCS

☐ NDA ☐ SOW ☐ ROE ☐ Approval ☐ 3rd Party ☐

/ENGAGEMENT

TYPE	SCOPE		TIMELINE
☐ Black Box	☐ Physical	☐ App	From:
	☐ Remote	☐ SocialEng	To:
☐ White Box	☐ Full-Spec	☐ RogueDevice	Status Updates:
	☐ Wireless	☐ Insider	_Daily _Weekly
☐ Grey Box	☐ WebApp	☐ DoS	_Monthly _Quarter

/CUSTOMER INFRASTRUCTURE

/TEST ACCOUNTS

/OBJECTIVES

/NOTES

/TEAM DATA

/TASKS

MEMBER	DESCRIPTION	FIN
		☐
		☐
		☐
		☐
		☐
		☐
		☐
		☐
		☐
		☐
		☐
		☐
		☐
		☐

/TOOLS

DATE	TYPE	NAME	DEPLOY LOCATION

/TEAM INFRASTRUCTURE

TYPE	IP/DOMAIN	USER/PASS

/TEAM ACCOUNTS

SERVICE	USERNAME	PASSWORD

/FINDINGS

/RECOMMENDATIONS

/CUSTOMER >

POC

POC

POC

/DOCS

☐ NDA ☐ SOW ☐ ROE ☐ Approval ☐ 3rd Party ☐

/ENGAGEMENT

TYPE	SCOPE		TIMELINE
☐ Black Box	☐ Physical	☐ App	From:
	☐ Remote	☐ SocialEng	To:
☐ White Box	☐ Full-Spec	☐ RogueDevice	Status Updates:
	☐ Wireless	☐ Insider	_Daily _Weekly
☐ Grey Box	☐ WebApp	☐ DoS	_Monthly _Quarter

/CUSTOMER INFRASTRUCTURE

/TEST ACCOUNTS

/OBJECTIVES

/NOTES

/TEAM DATA

/TASKS

MEMBER	DESCRIPTION	FIN
		☐
		☐
		☐
		☐
		☐
		☐
		☐
		☐
		☐
		☐
		☐
		☐
		☐
		☐

/TOOLS

DATE	TYPE	NAME	DEPLOY LOCATION

/TEAM INFRASTRUCTURE

TYPE	IP/DOMAIN	USER/PASS

/TEAM ACCOUNTS

SERVICE	USERNAME	PASSWORD

/FINDINGS

/RECOMMENDATIONS

/CUSTOMER >

POC

POC

POC

/DOCS

☐ NDA ☐ SOW ☐ ROE ☐ Approval ☐ 3rd Party ☐

/ENGAGEMENT

TYPE	SCOPE		TIMELINE
☐ Black Box	☐ Physical	☐ App	From:
	☐ Remote	☐ SocialEng	To:
☐ White Box	☐ Full-Spec	☐ RogueDevice	Status Updates:
	☐ Wireless	☐ Insider	_Daily _Weekly
☐ Grey Box	☐ WebApp	☐ DoS	_Monthly _Quarter

/CUSTOMER INFRASTRUCTURE

/TEST ACCOUNTS

/OBJECTIVES

/NOTES

/TEAM DATA

/TASKS

MEMBER	DESCRIPTION	FIN
		☐
		☐
		☐
		☐
		☐
		☐
		☐
		☐
		☐
		☐
		☐
		☐
		☐
		☐

/TOOLS

DATE	TYPE	NAME	DEPLOY LOCATION

/TEAM INFRASTRUCTURE

TYPE	IP/DOMAIN	USER/PASS

/TEAM ACCOUNTS

SERVICE	USERNAME	PASSWORD

/FINDINGS

/RECOMMENDATIONS

/CUSTOMER >

POC

POC

POC

/DOCS

☐NDA ☐ SOW ☐ ROE ☐Approval ☐ 3rd Party ☐

/ENGAGEMENT

TYPE	SCOPE		TIMELINE
☐ Black Box	☐ Physical	☐ App	From:
	☐ Remote	☐ SocialEng	To:
☐ White Box	☐ Full-Spec	☐ RogueDevice	Status Updates:
	☐ Wireless	☐ Insider	_Daily _Weekly
☐ Grey Box	☐ WebApp	☐ DoS	_Monthly _Quarter

/CUSTOMER INFRASTRUCTURE

/TEST ACCOUNTS

/OBJECTIVES

/NOTES

/TEAM DATA

/TASKS

MEMBER	DESCRIPTION	FIN
		☐
		☐
		☐
		☐
		☐
		☐
		☐
		☐
		☐
		☐
		☐
		☐
		☐
		☐

/TOOLS

DATE	TYPE	NAME	DEPLOY LOCATION

/TEAM INFRASTRUCTURE

TYPE	IP/DOMAIN	USER/PASS

/TEAM ACCOUNTS

SERVICE	USERNAME	PASSWORD

/FINDINGS

/RECOMMENDATIONS

/CUSTOMER >

POC

POC

POC

/DOCS

☐ NDA ☐ SOW ☐ ROE ☐ Approval ☐ 3rd Party ☐

/ENGAGEMENT

TYPE	SCOPE		TIMELINE
☐ Black Box	☐ Physical	☐ App	From:
	☐ Remote	☐ SocialEng	To:
☐ White Box	☐ Full-Spec	☐ RogueDevice	Status Updates:
	☐ Wireless	☐ Insider	_Daily _Weekly
☐ Grey Box	☐ WebApp	☐ DoS	_Monthly _Quarter

/CUSTOMER INFRASTRUCTURE

/TEST ACCOUNTS

/OBJECTIVES

/NOTES

/TEAM DATA

/TASKS

MEMBER	DESCRIPTION	FIN
		☐
		☐
		☐
		☐
		☐
		☐
		☐
		☐
		☐
		☐
		☐
		☐
		☐
		☐

/TOOLS

DATE	TYPE	NAME	DEPLOY LOCATION

/TEAM INFRASTRUCTURE

TYPE	IP/DOMAIN	USER/PASS

/TEAM ACCOUNTS

SERVICE	USERNAME	PASSWORD

/FINDINGS

/RECOMMENDATIONS

/CUSTOMER >

POC

POC

POC

/DOCS

☐ NDA ☐ SOW ☐ ROE ☐ Approval ☐ 3rd Party ☐

/ENGAGEMENT

TYPE	SCOPE		TIMELINE
☐ Black Box	☐ Physical	☐ App	From:
	☐ Remote	☐ SocialEng	To:
☐ White Box	☐ Full-Spec	☐ RogueDevice	Status Updates:
	☐ Wireless	☐ Insider	_Daily _Weekly
☐ Grey Box	☐ WebApp	☐ DoS	_Monthly _Quarter

/CUSTOMER INFRASTRUCTURE

/TEST ACCOUNTS

/OBJECTIVES

/NOTES

/TEAM DATA

/TASKS

MEMBER	DESCRIPTION	FIN
		☐
		☐
		☐
		☐
		☐
		☐
		☐
		☐
		☐
		☐
		☐
		☐
		☐
		☐

/TOOLS

DATE	TYPE	NAME	DEPLOY LOCATION

/TEAM INFRASTRUCTURE

TYPE	IP/DOMAIN	USER/PASS

/TEAM ACCOUNTS

SERVICE	USERNAME	PASSWORD

/FINDINGS

/RECOMMENDATIONS

/CUSTOMER >

POC

POC

POC

/DOCS

☐ NDA ☐ SOW ☐ ROE ☐ Approval ☐ 3rd Party ☐

/ENGAGEMENT

TYPE	SCOPE		TIMELINE
☐ Black Box	☐ Physical	☐ App	From:
	☐ Remote	☐ SocialEng	To:
☐ White Box	☐ Full-Spec	☐ RogueDevice	Status Updates:
	☐ Wireless	☐ Insider	_Daily _Weekly
☐ Grey Box	☐ WebApp	☐ DoS	_Monthly _Quarter

/CUSTOMER INFRASTRUCTURE

/TEST ACCOUNTS

/OBJECTIVES

/NOTES

/TEAM DATA

/TASKS

MEMBER	DESCRIPTION	FIN
		☐
		☐
		☐
		☐
		☐
		☐
		☐
		☐
		☐
		☐
		☐
		☐
		☐
		☐

/TOOLS

DATE	TYPE	NAME	DEPLOY LOCATION

/TEAM INFRASTRUCTURE

TYPE	IP/DOMAIN	USER/PASS

/TEAM ACCOUNTS

SERVICE	USERNAME	PASSWORD

/FINDINGS

/RECOMMENDATIONS

/CUSTOMER >

POC

POC

POC

/DOCS

☐ NDA ☐ SOW ☐ ROE ☐ Approval ☐ 3rd Party ☐

/ENGAGEMENT

TYPE	SCOPE		TIMELINE
☐ Black Box	☐ Physical	☐ App	From:
	☐ Remote	☐ SocialEng	To:
☐ White Box	☐ Full-Spec	☐ RogueDevice	Status Updates:
	☐ Wireless	☐ Insider	_Daily _Weekly
☐ Grey Box	☐ WebApp	☐ DoS	_Monthly _Quarter

/CUSTOMER INFRASTRUCTURE

/TEST ACCOUNTS

/OBJECTIVES

/NOTES

/TEAM DATA

/TASKS

MEMBER	DESCRIPTION	FIN
		☐
		☐
		☐
		☐
		☐
		☐
		☐
		☐
		☐
		☐
		☐
		☐
		☐
		☐

/TOOLS

DATE	TYPE	NAME	DEPLOY LOCATION

/TEAM INFRASTRUCTURE

TYPE	IP/DOMAIN	USER/PASS

/TEAM ACCOUNTS

SERVICE	USERNAME	PASSWORD

/FINDINGS

/RECOMMENDATIONS

/CUSTOMER >

POC

POC

POC

/DOCS

☐ NDA ☐ SOW ☐ ROE ☐ Approval ☐ 3rd Party ☐

/ENGAGEMENT

TYPE	SCOPE		TIMELINE
☐ Black Box	☐ Physical	☐ App	From:
	☐ Remote	☐ SocialEng	To:
☐ White Box	☐ Full-Spec	☐ RogueDevice	Status Updates:
	☐ Wireless	☐ Insider	_Daily _Weekly
☐ Grey Box	☐ WebApp	☐ DoS	_Monthly _Quarter

/CUSTOMER INFRASTRUCTURE

/TEST ACCOUNTS

/OBJECTIVES

/NOTES

/TEAM DATA

/TASKS

MEMBER	DESCRIPTION	FIN
		☐
		☐
		☐
		☐
		☐
		☐
		☐
		☐
		☐
		☐
		☐
		☐
		☐
		☐

/TOOLS

DATE	TYPE	NAME	DEPLOY LOCATION

/TEAM INFRASTRUCTURE

TYPE	IP/DOMAIN	USER/PASS

/TEAM ACCOUNTS

SERVICE	USERNAME	PASSWORD

/FINDINGS

/RECOMMENDATIONS

/CUSTOMER >

POC

POC

POC

/DOCS

☐NDA ☐ SOW ☐ ROE ☐Approval ☐ 3rd Party ☐

/ENGAGEMENT

TYPE	SCOPE		TIMELINE
☐ Black Box	☐ Physical	☐ App	From:
	☐ Remote	☐ SocialEng	To:
☐ White Box	☐ Full-Spec	☐ RogueDevice	Status Updates:
	☐ Wireless	☐ Insider	_Daily _Weekly
☐ Grey Box	☐ WebApp	☐ DoS	_Monthly _Quarter

/CUSTOMER INFRASTRUCTURE

/TEST ACCOUNTS

/OBJECTIVES

/NOTES

/TEAM DATA

/TASKS

MEMBER	DESCRIPTION	FIN
		☐
		☐
		☐
		☐
		☐
		☐
		☐
		☐
		☐
		☐
		☐
		☐
		☐
		☐

/TOOLS

DATE	TYPE	NAME	DEPLOY LOCATION

/TEAM INFRASTRUCTURE

TYPE	IP/DOMAIN	USER/PASS

/TEAM ACCOUNTS

SERVICE	USERNAME	PASSWORD

/FINDINGS

/RECOMMENDATIONS

/CONTACTS

NAME	#
EMAIL	
NAME	#
EMAIL	
NAME	#
EMAIL	
NAME	#
EMAIL	
NAME	#
EMAIL	
NAME	#
EMAIL	
NAME	#
EMAIL	
NAME	#
EMAIL	
NAME	#
EMAIL	
NAME	#
EMAIL	
NAME	#
EMAIL	
NAME	#
EMAIL	
NAME	#
EMAIL	
NAME	#
EMAIL	

/CONTACTS

NAME	#
EMAIL	
NAME	#
EMAIL	
NAME	#
EMAIL	
NAME	#
EMAIL	
NAME	#
EMAIL	
NAME	#
EMAIL	
NAME	#
EMAIL	
NAME	#
EMAIL	
NAME	#
EMAIL	
NAME	#
EMAIL	
NAME	#
EMAIL	
NAME	#
EMAIL	
NAME	#
EMAIL	
NAME	#
EMAIL	

/CONTACTS

NAME	**#**
EMAIL	
NAME	**#**
EMAIL	
NAME	**#**
EMAIL	
NAME	**#**
EMAIL	
NAME	**#**
EMAIL	
NAME	**#**
EMAIL	
NAME	**#**
EMAIL	
NAME	**#**
EMAIL	
NAME	**#**
EMAIL	
NAME	**#**
EMAIL	
NAME	**#**
EMAIL	
NAME	**#**
EMAIL	
NAME	**#**
EMAIL	
NAME	**#**
EMAIL	

/CONTACTS

NAME	**#**
EMAIL	
NAME	**#**
EMAIL	
NAME	**#**
EMAIL	
NAME	**#**
EMAIL	
NAME	**#**
EMAIL	
NAME	**#**
EMAIL	
NAME	**#**
EMAIL	
NAME	**#**
EMAIL	
NAME	**#**
EMAIL	
NAME	**#**
EMAIL	
NAME	**#**
EMAIL	
NAME	**#**
EMAIL	
NAME	**#**
EMAIL	
NAME	**#**
EMAIL	

/CONTACTS

NAME	**#**
EMAIL	
NAME	**#**
EMAIL	
NAME	**#**
EMAIL	
NAME	**#**
EMAIL	
NAME	**#**
EMAIL	
NAME	**#**
EMAIL	
NAME	**#**
EMAIL	
NAME	**#**
EMAIL	
NAME	**#**
EMAIL	
NAME	**#**
EMAIL	
NAME	**#**
EMAIL	
NAME	**#**
EMAIL	
NAME	**#**
EMAIL	
NAME	**#**
EMAIL	

Made in the USA
Monee, IL
04 November 2026

67376796R00105